Many Lives in One

Based on a True Story

Sintia Lazo

ISBN 978-1-64140-492-1 (paperback)
ISBN 978-1-64140-493-8 (digital)

Copyright © 2018 by Sintia Lazo

All rights reserved. No part of this publication may be reproduced, distributed, or transmitted in any form or by any means, including photocopying, recording, or other electronic or mechanical methods without the prior written permission of the publisher. For permission requests, solicit the publisher via the address below.

Christian Faith Publishing, Inc.
832 Park Avenue
Meadville, PA 16335
www.christianfaithpublishing.com

Printed in the United States of America

CHAPTER 1

Footprint of a Girl

Her name is July, and she wanted to write this story for those girls, teenagers, and woman, who at some point in their lives had no reason to continue living after what happened to them.

In July's opinion, there is always a higher power, or however you want to call it, who is making you stronger. But if you are a believer of God like July or have lost faith at some point, maybe this story may change your mind on who God is and how his power works. Please have an open mind of what you about to read.

For as long as July remembers, life was hard to understand. She was a special three-year-old girl. She survived a deadly incident where she almost drowned while she was playing with her cousin in a water well. Her cousin was the same age as her. The incident occurred when they were trying to get a toy from the water well. The unexpected happened when July's cousin first tried to grab the toy and she drowned in the process. July survived and her cousin died. July and her family tried to understand how this sad incident happened. The sorrow in the whole family was too much, and they were inconsolable.

So here was July's first footprint—she survived a deadly incident.

In the course of July's life, she was told that she was an unwanted child by her parents. They would say to July that she was an accident. July question if her mother and dad wished that she was the one who died that day at the water well. On top of that, things were horrible as she grew up in a house with her two brothers and a domineering father who would hit them for not doing the chores around the house. For example, when July forgot to feed her little brothers. Also, he hit her once when she was only six years old. He threw her from the second floor, and July rolled down the stairs. Then he hit her with the belt. Her mother couldn't help July because he would beat her too. One day he stuck some scissor on her mother's thigh and left her unable to walk for a few days. Thankfully, she recuperated. He was a clothes designer and used to design man's suits. He had a good business running. They were an ordinary family. Everything was provided for them: a nice house and money. But then July's dad got too greedy and wanted to expand his business and move to another country.

Not surprisingly, they got a divorce. Well, it didn't hurt much at the moment because on the long run it was best for everyone's safety. Lamentably, he left behind three little kids—a six-month-old little boy named Dani, a three-year-old little boy named Angel, and a six-year-old little girl named July. It was a bittersweet moment for July. She wanted him gone, but she loves him at the same time. Sadly, since then they never saw him again. And it will accumulate pain in the course of the years because after all, he was their dad.

July's second footprint—not having a father. He completely disappeared from their life.

Her grandmother, the mom of her dad, felt guilty that her son left them and started taking of care of them. She was a Christian old lady and proud to have two daughters who married pastors and gracefully have their church. July's grandmother would take July and her brothers to their church, and that was the first time, at the age of six years old, that she stepped foot in a church. General speaking, it felt weird when she saw people praying, dancing, and clapping with their hands. July didn't understand, but on the contrary, she felt calm from all the pain she was feeling from her dad's leaving. And that's what Christians call the Holy Spirit. Unexplainably, the Holy Spirit was touching her without her knowing. This explains the special power that July had always felt around her. It has protected her since she was little girl from death and problems. It was like a great force was surrounding her. Also, one thing July never told anybody during all the commotion. She can see shadows and hear stuff. She knew it wasn't normal, but she continued with her life like that.

July's mother, however, needed to work to feed her children, so she did. In the beginning, she would leave her kids unsupervised. Since July was the oldest, she had the role of taking care of her brothers like a mother would. She would take Angel to kindergarten school and shower them and feed them. But because of this situation, the family was forced to move in with their grandmother. Unfortunately, their mom couldn't keep up with the business that their dad left them to maintain the house and make payments for the bills. Eventually, they lost the business and were financially broke. Because of this, they need a new place to live.

July life changed completely when she and brothers moved to live with her grandmother and uncle. She thought things were going to be safer. On the contrary, things got worse. She was abused by her uncle when she was six years old. At that time July thought this was normal. Remember she was only six years, and no one knew. She never told anybody because she felt ashamed. But one day her grandmother found him in the act. July was naked on the bed, and it was the first time he was going to penetrate her. But he wasn't able to because just at the right time, her grandmother walks in on him. She got so angry that she put a chair with a rope around his neck. July cried in the corner, terrified. She realized that what he was doing to her wasn't normal. Then her grandmother got him out and told him if he tries to do it again she was going to kill him. Then she went and asked July if she was okay. She got her dressed and explained to her that he wasn't in his right mind and that was the reason for what he had done to her. She said she would make sure he never do it again. But it did happen again until the age of nine, but she never found out.

July's third footprint of her life was being abused by her uncle for three years. Sadly she was going to carry that for the rest of her life.

Those three years hurt the relationship between July and her mom because she was never there. She was always working. That's why July blamed her mother for what happened to her and her brothers.

At the age of nine July turns into a little rebel against her mother. There was no trust between them, and there was no hope for her and her brothers because at this point it was certain that they were going to grow up without a mother too.

In addition to that, their mom remarries and they were going to move with their stepdad. They stop going to church because their grandmother didn't approve of this new relation of her mom with this other man. Also, it was too soon to move the kids to live with him. Unfortunately, their grandmother was right because not after three months of living with this guy, he started hitting July and her brother. The excuse of their mom was that he was disciplining them. She also told them to call him Dad. It was confusing to them.

Thankfully, he decides to move to another country for a better life opportunity. Their mom was devastated because she was in love with him and didn't want him to go. But then he went anyway. Not after six months of him leaving, another decision of their mom (Alba) would make July mature at just nine years old. When her mother decided to follow her significant other, she was not thinking right by leaving her kids behind. As a matter fact her excuse was the same as him. She was leaving for a better job opportunity. Generally speaking, she didn't care about leaving her children with some people that her kids didn't know before—an uncle with five kids.

When they finally move in with them, immediately July, just nine years old, learned how cook and to clean for all twelve people living in the house. July practically lived the Cinderella story, cleaning and cooking for all those people. Their cousin would bully them by saying to July and her brother that nobody wanted them, not even their mom. These were very hurtful words that got to them, and it was hard to understand that their mother left them for a man. Then July and her brother started going to the Catholic church. They went to an Evangelist church with their grandmother before. The different between the religions didn't matter to them because it felt like an escape from all the drama in their life. July felt that God was there with her, not because of the religion but because she prayed a lot to him. It also felt like he was consoling her and her brothers. July remembers that the church had many activities that they enjoyed and liked. For that reason, they had their first Communion and got baptized. They also attended classes to accomplished them. July was eleven and her brother Angel was eight when they got baptized. It was a beautiful day. They played, ate, and had so much fun. The place was teaching them that there was still hope for them. The place where they lived was on the mountain. The view was peaceful. July used to pray a lot to God, asking him for her mom to come back to them. She also prayed for their dad, but deep inside she didn't care much about him.

All of a sudden, one day, they received a phone call from their mom. After three years of not knowing what was going to happen to them, it was an emotional moment. When July grab the phone, she cried like she never cried before. She couldn't even talk to her mom. Her mother asked her what happened. Then July answered in between the crying, "I'm not happy here because these people are treating us wrong." Her mom said, "Sorry, baby, but I'm not ready to come back for you guys yet, but I will fix the problem." July hanged up the phone not knowing what her mom meant with what she said.

Soon after that, to their surprise, they talked on the phone again. Her mom told them that she was sending her sister to take them away from that place. The problem was their mom would send money to their uncle to feed them and dressed them but they were not doing that. They were keeping the money for themselves. July and her brothers remember eating beans every day for the three-course meal throughout the three years they lived with them. So July and her brothers never had a good meal or good clothes. They thought their mom had forgotten them. Their mom was so angry. But this family was so greedy with the money they're getting for taking care of kids that they didn't want to give them away. But their mom got a letter sign by lawyer saying that she was giving full custody to their aunt and that's how they were finally free from these family.

July and her brothers moved again with their aunt. Well, it was the same thing again. Nobody wanted them. Here they go again, trying to fit in, uncertain of when their mom would come back for them. The only satisfaction they had was that they could talk with their mom on the phone, and their mom was responsible this time by sending money to them for food and clothes. She promised that it would be soon that they would see each other again and be together again.

Fortunately, they went back to the Evangelic church and enrolled at a Christian school. It was fun. Once again this was an escape for July and her brothers. At this point, they were a little confused because of change of religion, but of course, they were at the right age to understand the difference of each faith. Most importantly, July and her brothers knew that it was the same *God* they were praising. The problem was that the Evangelic family was so angry because they got baptized and did their first communion through the Catholic church. Their family forgot that July and her brothers were just following rules, and they felt no regret by attending the Catholic religion.

Two years went by, and there was still no word from their mother. At this point, they were resigned to the fact that their mother was never going to come back for them.

The fourth footprint was accepting that they were orphans and nobody wanted them. Their dad completely disappeared from their life. He never came back for them, and their mom was doing the same.

At this time, July and her brothers only hope was to hold on to their mom's word that she coming back for them. It was their only strength.

Finally, the day came for July and her brother to see their mother again. After five years of not having her around, they couldn't believe they were on their way to be reunited with their mom. Their emotion was everywhere and a little awkward, but they were happy. For some reason, things were going to change quickly because they never had a relationship together.

CHAPTER 2

Footprint of a Teenager

For the most part, everybody was happy they were back together with their mom. But, of course, the big elephant between them was their stepdad because they never got along with him back when they lived together before. They never had a good relationship with him, and he was probably feeling the same way too. In contrary, their mom acted like everything was normal. She wanted everyone to get along. On the other hand, they were excited with all the new clothes they got and even eating cereal felt good at the moment. For the most part, everything was perfect and everybody was getting along just as their mom wanted.

July was fourteen years old in middle school, and her brothers were in elementary. It was tough because of the language barrier. However, they tried hard to do good in school. As always, the unexpected happened. July felt a sharp pain in her lower belly, and she asked to go the bathroom. She saw blood in her underwear and then quickly asked to call her mom so she could pick her up from school. July remembers not going to school for three days because of the severe pain. The doctors told her that it was because her period came late and it caused the pain to be intense. The doctor gave her painkiller. For as long as she can remember, the pain stayed the same.

In the meantime, they were going to church from time to time. After church, they would go to a restaurant to have lunch. That was one of the good memories July and her brothers would hold close to their heart. Considering the fact of their situation with their stepdad was not good, they tried to be a family. But it was a matter of time before things changed at a blink of an eye.

After one year, their mom got pregnant with another little brother for July. It was more responsibility around the house. Thank God for his arrival because it brought the family a little closer together. They were very excited about him, but July's life suddenly would take another wrong turn.

After another year July started high school and made friends her age. They were very mature for July because they were already having sex at the age of fifteen. Of course, at lunch, that's all they would talk about. They asked July if she ever had sex, and she answered no. When July told them that she was a virgin, they laughed at her.

July was trying to enjoy her teenage years. She liked a boy from her class, and they got together. It was a very innocent relationship. They pop kissed, they held hands, but that would be the last good memory she would have as a teenager because things were going to change quickly. Her friends bullied July by saying that she was having sex with her boyfriend when it was not true. July felt so ashamed and moved to another school.

Another bad turn for July was that they didn't have much money. So they decided to move to an efficiency one bedroom, one bathroom, and small tiny kitchen for six people it was a little place to live and the reason for moving to a smaller place was to save money in order to buy a house. After that July's little brother was born, and they were happy with him. One day her stepdad invited a friend he barely knew to a barbecue they were having. After that day this man would come to the efficiency three times at week for months. July knew that he was trying to find ways to sit by her side, and he always did it when no one was looking. Of course, July ignored him and would always walk away from him and go where her mom or her stepdad can see her. But the guy acted like he was going their way to help them. This went on for three months, and July always ignored him. But he got obsessed with her, it was scary. The most twisted part of all was that this guy had a wife with a one-year-old baby. He wasn't well in his mind. On the other hand, July and her mom were arguing a lot. July needed to help her mother more around the house, but instead, she won't listen and would still go out with friends, sometimes friends from church. As a result, her mom would get angry for not doing what July was told and she got punished. With one week to go with her work, July didn't want to go with her. Instead she had a plan. July proposed to her mom that if she wanted her to help, she would stay and babysit her little brother while she worked. July's mom agreed. It was a big mistake they made because one day of that week when July was babysitting her little brother, the crazy man came by the house. It was 1:00 p.m. and July remembers the knock on the door. When she asked who was it, it was the crazy man who answered back, saying, "Your mom send me to give something." July opened the door. When she saw him, July got so scared. She quickly tried to close the door on him, but he was stronger than her. July knew she was in trouble. Everything was so close, and he quickly pushed her against the refrigerator, then to the sofa, and from there to the bed. Her little brother cried in his crib while the guy forced her to have sex with him and at the same time taking her virginity away. When he finished and moved away on top of her, July ran to the bathroom and locked herself inside. She cried, but then he followed her and said from across the door, "Open the door. Everything is going to be okay. Supposedly in his head, it was to calm July down.

He would tell her, "I'm twenty-three-year old man. I would take care of you, and if you get pregnant, don't worry our baby is going to be beautiful. I'm going to married you."

July cried from across the door. She threatened him by saying that she would tell her stepdad and her mom what he had done to her. Therefore he needed to leave. She also remembered that her brothers were on their way to the house from school. She made sure he knew that too, and she screamed, "My brothers are on their way from school, and they are going to caught you." Meanwhile, from across the room, her little brother was still crying and that was all July was hearing. So July slowly opened the door. Finally, he left. More importantly, from then on, he never came back to the house. She never heard from him again. He disappeared, and unfortunately, he was not caught.

When she came out the bathroom, she made sure her little brother calm down. Then July went to the other room to pray, telling God why this incident happened to her and to help her understand the reason why. July felt like God had left her or she was the one who left him, and probably that's why this happened to her. At that time July was not attending church, only from time to time. Was that her sin? Not being fully committed to God, July had so many questions.

The first footprint as a teenager—she lost her virginity by rape.

One month passed and July went to church, because after all, she believed in God. She was invited to a retreat where she got baptized through the Evangelic religion because last time her family got angry at July when she got baptized by the Catholic faith. Well, this time she was fifteen years old. She understood why she was getting baptized, and the experience was beautiful. When she was coming up from the water, she saw a white light and felt pure. July made friends and told some people what happened to her. She was concerned that she could be pregnant because her period was late for a month. Well, with that said, they got back from the retreat. A week passed, and somebody told her mom. Soon after July's mom asked her if this was true. July said yes.

The second footprint was she got pregnant by rape.

Obviously, she was going to have the baby, but after two months, July was having problems with the pregnancy. Her mom took her to the emergency room where the doctor told her that she was losing the baby. July went back home with a high fever and lower belly pain that lasted a month. She almost died, but through the grace of God, she didn't.

After that, the church she attended was right because the pastor leading the church was wise. He was also a missionary, so he was called to leave to another country. Leaving his younger son to lead the church at the beginning he was doing a good job, but some teenagers would take advantage of him, suggesting to him to make the church a younger version. It got out control that sometimes they would do wrong things. They also took advantage of July's situation. Instead of comforting her, they would offer her alcohol and two of them tried to be friends with July just to have sex with her. But July's mom knew something was wrong with the church and that July was getting worse and acting out, and like always July didn't want to listen to her mom. July blamed her for leaving her and her brothers alone for many years and for what happened to her recently.

July stopped going to church and focused on her studies. She earned three medals in junior year. But in between being good in school, she would go out with friends and drink heavily, even went clubbing. July knew that her faith wasn't gone, and she also knew that what she was doing was wrong. Although, in the midst of it all, God was protecting her from all the mistakes she was making, even from those she didn't do and was blamed for them. July still needed to learn from her mistake because God was there even when she thought no one was there for her. God was going to show her the way.

Her mom finally saved some money to buy a beautiful house with a pool, but July was hurting so much that not even this house brought her happiness to her. Soon her senior year would come to an end, and one of her friends set up a blind date for her. But July told him that she didn't want any relationship with nobody, that she could believe in love anymore. However, she agreed to meet with this blind date. July thought it was going to be the same as others, just a game. But it turned to be a bittersweet situation. The reason being that her stepdad was taking in his role as a dad seriously by telling her what to do and sometimes jealous. Worse of all, her mother also let him hit July and her brother. July's anger accumulated against him, and July yelled at him all the time, "You not my dad and never going to be." July felt that he was a monster because he wouldn't stop hitting them. With this in mind, July asked her mother for permission to go out on this blind date and her mother said yes, but with the condition that the date should be during lunchtime. July agreed. But July's stepdad was in the house when July was getting ready to leave.

Her stepdad asked, "Where are you going? You never ask me for permission to get out this house, especially for a date."

July answered, "Yes, I had asked my mom for permission. If you want we can call her right now…"

And so they did. After hearing July's mom telling him that it was okay for July to go, he got so upset and still didn't want July to go anywhere. With her mother still on the phone and July's date at the door waiting for her, July started walking toward the door. Her stepdad grabs her by the hair, sweeping the floor with her and at the same time punching her in the face. July started bleeding from her mouth. July never hung up the phone with her mom, and the blind date, seeing this crazy event, called the police. July's mom heard that the police was on the way. In disbelief of what was happening, July's mom arrived at the same time the police reached the house. July thought her mom was there to rescue her. Instead, she was furious at July and told her to go and tell the cops that her stepdad was disciplining her. The worst part was that her mother never asked July if she was okay. With everything going on, July's mom forgot that the blind date was still there and that he was the one who called the police and saw everything. So he was telling the contrary to the police. So the police took July aside and told her, "Six months from now you will turn eighteen years old. And if you say what you mother wants right now, then later you are not going to have the opportunity to put him in jail and charge him with child abuse. This is your only chance." But July obeyed her mom. She just didn't want her mom to be angry at her, so the police left. July, mad at her mom, ran off with her blind date. She was disappointed at her mom for taking her stepdad's side and for not asking her if she was okay.

Third footprint—she was betrayed by her mother.

The blind date took advantage of the situation. He was good with words by comforting her, respecting her and with time July thought she was in love with him, and little by little he convinced her to leave her mom to go away with him. July was close to graduating, but things were not getting better at her house with her stepdad and her mom. July's mom was always taking his side. It was impossible to have a conversation with her mom. Having said that, July made the wrong decision to leave her brothers and her mom and went to live with her boyfriend. She left without saying good-bye to no one, just left a brief letter, saying, "I can't take it no more. You don't believe anything I said. Sorry, I have to go."

Deciding on leaving her life behind, she thought that she had a chance with this guy and that she was going to have a good future with him. Of course, life turned into a complicated situation that it would make her think twice about her decision of leaving her family behind. For an instant she was close to death once again. At this point, July has forgotten about God altogether. When driving away with her boyfriend to another state, July looks up the sky and felt alone. She convince her self that by moving away it would help her leave her past behind to finally move forward and start a fresh new life. At seventeen years old, she felt like an adult turning into a woman. To sum up, she was feeling guilty for knowing God and not asking him about this decision she was making. She knew that whatever mistake she makes from now on as a woman, it would be on her one by one, which it was going to be like a roller coaster ride for July.

CHAPTER 3

Footprint of a Mid-woman

July believed that her life was going to change for the good. Her only regret was leaving her brothers behind as they were like her kids when they were growing up.

After all she only knew her boyfriend for only five months, but July felt that he could help in the situation she was in. She had a slight doubt about him being a good man for her in the future, but there was no other way to get out from the problem with her family. She tried to ask another family to help her and explain what was happened to her, but they stabbed her on her back by telling her mother that she went to them for help. July's mom got furious with July for going to them and telling them the problems in their house. July's mom wanted it to keep it secret, so that was why there was no option but to go with her boyfriend. It was like two sharp edges of a knife. On one hand July could stay with her mom and continue suffering, and on another side, she leaves with her boyfriend she barely knew, taking a leap of faith that it would go well with him so she can escape from her suffering.

For starters, when arriving at his mom's house, they offered them a room. Meanwhile, they found a job, and eventually moved out to start a life together as a couple.

One month passed of her applying for jobs, and thankfully one came through for July. A retail company hired her as a cashier. It was a good paying job for her. Meanwhile, her boyfriend was still without a job, and that was when July found out one of his secrets. He didn't like to work, and he couldn't get a job anywhere and couldn't keep one for a long term. As a matter fact after six months had passed, he was still without a job. Thank God his mom liked July because she would have thrown him out long ago. By the seventh month, problems with him started to feel like hell, because in those seven months they fought a lot and he began to hit July.

What karma isn't for this reason: July moved out of her house, practically speaking, and moved from one nightmare to relive another.

But his boyfriend's father came on July's defense two times when he saw him hitting her.

Thankfully, July had money save up for an apartment, so she moved out, leaving him with his mom.

When she moved to her new apartment, July felt the Holy Spirit was there with her because, unconsciously, July started buying angel statues. And from then on July made it her hobby to collect angel status. She also bought a Bible and had it opened in her room. What do you know? God was there in her darkest hours when she alone with no family or friends to help her. God made it clear that he was there with her and for some reason, July couldn't forget about him too.

The truth was that July had been searching for love her whole life from any human being. Since she was little, this was her problem. Besides, even when she was going through so much in her life, she couldn't feel anything bad or think anything bad against the people who hurt her. It was the opposite. July was the sweetest girl with everybody and was always trying to help if she could. She was also a very compassionate person.

For this reason, she thought it was best to give her boyfriend another chance. He promised her that he was going to change. He did, and for the two years they were married, he had a stable job. Everything started to change when he wanted children. July not so much. Still, she kept an open mind about it. God knew thing were going to change, and it did. He started going out with friends, and one day brought people to the house and was doing drugs with them, which it was unacceptable for July. Of course, July threw them out and that's when he got angry and hit her, leaving her with a black eye and her arms and legs in bruises. She didn't go to work for three days, and the next four days she tried to cover up her purple eye with makeup. But still people knew at work, and the neighbors also knew because they heard July scream, and all them tried to help July. But he was so good at convincing people that it was an accident that he didn't mean to do it. This went on for six months. As consequence, July tried one time to do drugs but she didn't like it. But she was drinking a lot. However, the Holy Spirit was there with her because she started having this thought in her head, asking her, *What are you doing? Do you want to do this for the rest of your life? You have to get out of this mess. Remember your God.* So she started praying to God.

For most people, this is your inner self talking to you or your gut telling you what to do. But in July's opinion is was God talking to her. July started to make a plan to escape, and like the prodigal son in the Bible says, she gathered enough strength to call her mom, asking her to take her back. July was twenty-one when she realized her mistake. Three years has passed, and they hadn't talked to each other. Her mother couldn't believe that it was July on the phone, and she answered, "Yes, I take you back." July then asked a coworker to give her a ride to the airport and booked a flight for 9:00 a.m. But there was a problem. The flight was too early. She needed to wait for him to leave for work at 8:00 a.m. And on top of that, he received a call, saying that he need not work that that day because it was raining. July's heart dropped. She couldn't believe what was happening. She was so nervous and was praying silently. And what did you know? He got called back at 8:20 a.m., saying that he was needed for work. Thank God! So July rushed to go to her coworker's car, hoping to arrive on time for her flight. July prayed the whole way to airport. Thankfully, she made it in time. Additionally, she was afraid of heights but she knew this was her only chance to escape. July left a letter explaining why she was leaving him and placed her wedding ring on top it.

In the other end, her mother was waiting at the airport for July.

When they first saw each other, no words were said but a hug, even when driving back to the house, not a word. July was happy she was going to see her brothers, but she was also afraid because she knew the rule of the house. Not shortly after July found out that their stepdad was hitting her brothers too, and it started after she left. Once again July started preparing her escape, and quickly, within a week, she got a job and saved money to move out because it was impossible to live in a house with that kind of environment. She was always fighting with her mom and her stepdad. There was no peace.

Little by little things progressed for July. She found a better job opportunity, and she was feeling a bit happier. Well, you would think she had already learned from her mistake and be a little conscious of how to go about life. But here she goes again, she continued making wrong decisions.

She met a guy and fell in love with him, her soul mate she would say. He also had the same problem like her ex-husband. He didn't like to work and couldn't keep one for a long term. Her mother didn't like him because of that. They move in together, and for one year July was paying all the bills. Unfortunately at this period she forgot about God. Not only that she also starting going to clubs with friends and drinking again. At the age of twenty-two, got pregnant with his baby, and because of the financial situation, she decided to have an abortion. It was a tough decision for her because kept it secret from him. She never mentioned it to him. Meanwhile, he was still without a job. Eight months passed, and nothing had changed, except that once again she got pregnant. This time she told him about it. She was worried. They discussed it, and they came to the conclusion that the main problem was him not having a job and how they could not raise a child without money and no car. He tried to look for a job, but it was like always on and off, nothing to show July that he was capable of raising a child. Then she went again this time with him by her side. She knew this wasn't a joke. And before two minutes going in with the precision, he asked, "July, are you sure?" She answered yes. However, July didn't measure the consequence on this decision because it cost their two-year relationship immediately after what they did. A month passed, and they both were struggling with the decision they made. Out of nowhere, one night, he left July without saying good- bye. July never saw it coming. She woke up one morning, and he wasn't there in bed by her side. So quickly she looked for him, then checked his closet. The clothes and everything of him were gone. She panicked and called her aunt for help. She couldn't believe it either. After two hours, July received a phone call. It was him asking to forgive him but that he wasn't coming back and to forget about him.

July was devastated. This was impossible in her mind. She gave him everything for two years. She thought they were soul mates in love. July had her heart broken. She needed answers, and there it was. He was hiding a big secret that July didn't know. He had a separate life with another woman. Yes, another woman. It hurt July so much to hear that. Unfortunately, she whet back to heavy drinking and at times drugs. She was missing class in college and left school. Someone told her about a place where she can earn more money as a dancer (not a stripper). It was a place where you can dance a regular song with clothes with a man for money and drink for money too. July tried it one night, and she made 350 dollars. No joke, in three days she made 1,000 dollars. So she quit her regular job and did this full time. She bought a beautiful car and had an apartment. She thought that this was going to erase her broken heart. But it only brought confusion, because she thought she was happy but she was only destroying her life. And many times she attempted to kill herself. Not to mention, the place where she work was very dangerous. If it weren't for God's mercy, she would be dead already. Of course, her mom didn't like what she was doing and stop talking with July for that reason. Then one day her brother Angel called and told July, "You have to come home. Our mom is taken by the police." July was surprised to hear that and drove there with doubts, but her brother was correct. July tried to go inside the house where the police were questioning her stepdad. This infuriated July, and she started screaming at him, "You are the one that supposes to be inside the squad car not our mom. You are the one who hit us. You are a hypocrite." The police escorted July out, telling her to calm down and forbade her to go back inside. Her stepdad was telling the police that July's mom was the one who hit him and probably yes she did it to defend herself. There is a saying, "Everything you do wrong will come back to you," and there was her mom paying for that day when she told

July just tell the cops he was disciplining her. It hurt to see when they took her away. The next day July's brother bailed her out from jail.

After that they met at July's apartment. Her mother didn't have a place to go, so they decided for her to stay with July at the apartment. It hurt to see her mother suffering so much, especially when July was going through something similar too. Two months passed, and they were still living together. One day July made a wrong decision of leaving with a date and was going to sleep over at his house. Fortunately, July's mom was there at the apartment to rescue her because this was one of those guys who adopted woman to turn them into prostitutes. July reacted when he was driving too far from what he said where they were going. After an hour they finally arrived, and certainly, it was a house filled with woman. July kept her calm and quickly called her mom to give her direction, and once again, beautiful God helped July's mom how to get there.

There is no explanation on how it happened. Because it was only one phone call that July made, and there was no GPS back then. Both of them can't explain how she got there. To conclude, she beeped the horn in front of the guy's house and the man was surprised and scared, asking how she found them. July responded, "That's my mom. If you don't let me go, she will call the cops." So the man let her go. July got in the car. Her mom was angry but was glad to see that July was okay.

They both came with a hypothesis that July's boyfriend needed to leave her so July could have the space to help her mom and for her mom had to go through the problem with her husband so she could help July on that day she was in danger. All in all, this is how God's work. He knew something bad was going to happen to July, and again, he made this whole master plan for so many years in order to have the right timing, the right moment, to help July. In the end, the best part is that they both came to an understanding that it was God's work.

But they forgot the first plan that God did all of that and they were brought back together because of it.

July's mom was confused with everything she was going through. She forgave her husband and went back to live with him. Yeah, love is strange, but she's a grown woman. July was once again alone in her apartment. One day a friend invited her to go to a Western rodeo. July agreed on going. It was one decision that was going to turn well for July, but only halfway because God wasn't done showing July his way.

CHAPTER 4

Footprint of a Woman

Without a doubt, going to the Western rodeo changed July's life altogether. Of course, there are some bombs on the road for her salvation with God, or like July likes to call it, make or break. With this in mind, July met the love of her life that day. It was like love at first sight. They laughed about everything like they knew each other for a long time. July kept it casual, but after a few weeks, she gave him her phone number. He called, and within a week, they began a friendship for three months. Then it turned into a relationship. July's mom was happy and approved of them being together. July and her mom were okay, but not entirely, because problems with her will come up again soon. Then July got pregnant. It wasn't planned, but they accepted God's plan to begin a new life together as a family by moving in together. At present, it didn't matter that they had different cultures and different religion. July is Evangelic, and he is Catholic. From both side of the family, they didn't approve either the culture or the religion. But there were in love, and that didn't matter to them. They always agree that if they both believe in God, nothing else matter and everything would be good. So they continued with their life together. They moved far away from both their families. They talked on the phone, but to avoid problems, they just distanced themselves a little bit.

Meanwhile, July prayed for her baby every month, especially when she knew she made many mistake in life and didn't want the baby to pay for her sin. Time passed, and it was time for July to have her baby. July's mother suggested that she was going to help her. But what July didn't know was that her mother had a different idea. July's mom picked her up to take her to the hospital. July's husband was on his way too. And as in old fashion lady, July's mom wanted July to have the baby the normal way and was making July push during her contractions until the doctors said that it was impossible for July to have the baby in the normal way. It was either her life or his. So they did a C-section, and instead of July's husband going inside with her, July's mom dictated that it was her that needed to go inside. When the baby came out, she took the child with her without July seeing the baby first. It was like she wanted July to suffer. When July was back in the room, she asked her husband where the baby was. Her husband said that her mom was taking care of him. July got so angry and yelled at her mother, "Who do that to another mother!" They got mad at each other again. When July finally saw her baby the first time, he had such beautiful blue eyes. He was so cute she fell in love with him. And because of what she went through when she was little, July took care of the baby like gold, most times overprotective. Sometimes the family was afraid of even touching the baby. They couldn't understand why July was acting like that and started talking bad about her. So July distanced herself from them again. Before a year passed, her mother tried to make peace with July. They celebrated his first birthday at her house, and things were so-so with her.

After two years July was planning to have her second child. July was praying for a girl, and God answered her prayer and gave her a girl. July was happy, and unfortunately, on her fourth month of pregnancy, she started bleeding. July rushed to see the doctors and did an ultrasound on her. Thank God the baby was fine. But next month she bled again and all the five months left of her pregnancy. Every month she has an ultrasound, and July prayed so much to God for her baby girl to be okay. He heard her prayers, and it was time to have the baby. Once again her mother wanted to help, and she wouldn't accept no for an answer. And like always she was making the decision for July. It was like she never realized the mistake she was making by taking away July and her husband the most beautiful memory in their life—seeing their kids come to life. But she didn't care or didn't listen and still went inside with July to have the baby. But the most important thing was that the baby was born in good health. Moments later July realized that for some reason she couldn't walk. The doctors needed to do surgery on her quickly, and for that she had stay in the hospital. July stayed on the hospital for some time without seeing her babies because her mom took them with her. When July finally came out of the hospital, July had it with her mother and took her children and left. July's mom started talking bad about July, telling people that July was going crazy overprotecting her babies. July's mom didn't have boundaries. It was whatever she wanted or nothing else.

Ever since July was little always trying to understand her mother's ways, but she makes it impossible to be at peace.

After a year July was thinking of looking for a job, but the kids were too small, so her husband said to wait a bit. Then July tried everything to do from home, but there was no success. She even tried to pick good furniture from the trash and sell them at the flea market. It worked, but it was hard work. After four years July started looking for a house that was approved. But because July didn't have a job and with only her husband's income, it wasn't enough. The bank said no, but the weird thing was, the realtor still proceeded with the process and July gave them the down payment. But later they didn't want to return the money to July. In fact, they lost it all. It was a disappointment. July decided to start looking for a job during the night or early morning so she could take care of the kids during the day and then maybe they could get approved in another try for the house. She found one. It wasn't a good pay job, but she kept it. Meanwhile, she was still looking for another one. An opportunity came through, but it was during the whole night, from 11:00 p.m. to 7:00 a.m. It paid well, so she took it.

Like any job at the beginning, they were looking weirdly at July. Along with that, there were rumors going around that apparently the lady who did the training had problems with everybody in there. In July, the second week of training, the woman wanted July get in trouble and to get her fired. Thankfully, there was proof that she had framed everything for July to get fired. Instead, this lady was the one who got fired. So July continued working there. The manager was a little harsh on her and made her cry a lot. July would go home crying every morning. July wanted to quit, but she reminded herself of the house she wanted to buy for her family. After five months, thing looks better but July finds something wrong about a coworker who was working there during the day. July reported to the manager, but it backfired for July. The coworker found out that it was July who went and told the manager and wanted to get revenge. One night a coworker was leaving the company, and they prepared a get-a-way party for her, and he was there. But July didn't know he was angry at her because he acted normal with July. They offered July a drink. She took it and cheered with them with one sip. After the second sip, July knew something was wrong and ran to her desk. But before she knew it, he caught up with her. He grabbed her by the mouth, and July passed out. There were flashes that she remembered when she tried escaping two times. July barely had the strength to walk, and he always caught up with her. She couldn't move fast. He raped her many time until the morning. When her husband went looking for July, all the coworkers and the manager tried covering him up because the company could get in trouble too. Her husband found July unconscious and carried her to the car. He was confused. But he did nothing and took her back to the house. The entire night and whole day July was unconscious. She could have died. When July came through, it was around five in the afternoon. Seconds after, she started throwing up. Then she received a phone call from a coworker who found out what happened to July. She saw the video where the guy appeared grabbing July. She told July that she was on her way to take to the hospital. July went with her to the hospital. The police came because it was a rape, and it is protocol when that happens. But when they went looking for the guy, the manager told that them he never worked there before, and he was never caught.

 In consequence, July's life changed. She drowned herself in alcohol and crying, asking God why? This brought back memories when she was raped as a girl, when she got raped as a teenager, and now as a woman. July would ask God, how much do you think I can take?

She was questioning God's purpose, and that's a no-no in God's eyes. But he was patient with July because he knew July would come to her senses. She managed not to drink during the day so she can take care of the kids. But she would often cry, and her boy would ask her, "What's wrong, Mom?" But she would always grab some strength and answer, "Nothing, baby, I'm okay." And every day since then he would ask July the same question even if she wasn't crying. He knew something wrong happened to his mom. Every night, as soon July put them to bed, the drinking would start for the whole night. It went on for two years. July struggled to have an ordinary life she couldn't go out to buy groceries or out to any store because this man knew where she lives and July was terrified he was looking for her to hurt her more. As a consequence, July looked twice everywhere she went. Frightened of everyone and everything that even a little noise would make her jump. She even called the police twice for imagining that someone was breaking into her house that make her nervous about everything, and for that reason she couldn't trust anyone. As for July's husband, he was assuming the worst of her. Because he blamed her for what happened that night. He didn't think it was a rape. He thought July had sex with this man just because. Even with all the proof he saw with his own eyes. He was mad with July for their marriage was crumbling. Because of the incident, July couldn't have sex with him as just to feel the touch of a man brought back memories. But one night he forces her to have sex with him, and July cried afterward. She couldn't believe why he did what he did, and for this reason, July added this to her list. She was raped by her husband too.

July was confused. She thought someone had put a curse on her. She has been through a lot since she was little, and she couldn't understand why God wasn't there that night to help her. She when to a lady to lift the curse. What a big mistake because this was going to anger God. July knew God but was losing faith in him. A regret July will carry with her for the rest of her life. And on top of all, the lady was charging her a lot of money every time July went, so July stopped the nonsense and went back to God.

A few month passed since that incident with her husband, and they were not talking with each other. Sadly, July's drinking continued but just on weekends. July couldn't stay married to her husband after what happened. So she decided to move out. She had some money saved. Then a realtor got her pre-approve for a house and went through the whole process again. But no luck. They also tried to stay with the money that she had already put down. But July got herself a lawyer and got it back. Her husband saw that she was serious in leaving him. He begged her to give him another chance, to not let him go. He even proposed that she marry him again. This time in front of God's eyes in the church because when they were married, they didn't have a proper wedding. July forgave him and accepted his proposal.

July was a bit happy, not completely, but was trying to stay focused. She entertained herself on doing the wedding on her own. It gave her hope. She was still drinking but less. After a long time not seeing her mom, she came back to her life. She wanted to help with the wedding, and this was a big mistake because she managed to convince July to do everything her way. It was just like she was the one getting married. She even wanted to buy a white dress to wear for her. July just wanted peace and allowed her do whatever she wanted. She didn't invite some family. They got angry with July because of it. The best thing she had brought back in July's life was a church that July fell in love with. July started going to this church, and that's the first time God spoke to July. That day will always be the most beautiful one. They had a beautiful wedding and had fun. Things were a little better in their relationship, but there were more problems to come up in their marriage.

July started going to the church her mother introduced her, but only on Sundays at first. Then July opened a retail clothing store, but her big mistake was not asking God before she opened the store. Because after a year she closed the store, not because it wasn't a success, but because the landlord was taking advantage of her. After seeing July succeeding so fast in six months, she wanted a lot more money for renting the place. But July wasn't going to take the bullying and closed the store. In all that one day, she was carrying the rent money with her. But before giving the money to the landlord, she went to Chinese restaurant and when she came out, she got robbed.

They took her purse with all the money in her wallet and all her credit cards. She was also carried her social card there too. This person when to her bank and took 5,000 dollars, making July's account negative. Not only that, her two kids' social number were there too. July got back home crying, asking God why? Explaining to him that she was just starting to be good on his path by going to church. But God always has a plan underneath it all.

Beyond words, July was driven by the church and was anxious to go back. The impact it left in her was that God was there even in those hard moments when she felt God wasn't there. But instead, July realized she was the one who left God. And for his mercy, July wanted to testify how she was alive. She cried when she told her story. She knew deep inside that God save her, but some people looked at her with judgment while other as brave. But July didn't care about what they would say about her, she felt at that moment like something was lifted from her shoulders. From then on July started worshipping and praising God when the Holy Spirit came through for her. And she began having a vision of angels. One angel look like a woman and bright like star. She was on top of a man who was praying with his arms up and moving up and down like a puppet. After the worship, July approached him to tell him what she saw and he agreed that something was pulling him up and down just like July described. Then she saw Jesus walking on the hallway. Then he moved to the stage where he started getting taller and bigger. Then he opened his arms, turning them into big white wings. He opened them to hug the entire church. Then she also had unexplainable dreams.

Once again her husband was going to betray her, but this time not alone. His sister and July's mom were his accomplices. July in previous times had problems with her sister-in-law, and July tried to stay away from her, but she insisted on seeing her nephews. July ask her if she could babysit them while July looked for a job, and her sister-in-law agreed. But things didn't work out that way. July's sister-in-law was the one who started working. Then she began getting along with July's mom. They both talk about how July was overprotecting her kids. And not only that, July's husband got involved and together the three of them bullied July to the point that they even wanted to take her children away. July quickly starting praying to God to tell him God this people wants to take my kids away please help me and show me the way, God they don't realize that they are not hurting me but the children by taking their mother away from them.

July has never prayed to God like she was doing during the time. She was so scared they will win this war they had against her of taking her kids away. Their big mistake was that they underestimated the power of God because July wasn't alone. God was with her.

When going through this war, July asked God for forgiveness for what she was about to do for they were family and it was going to hurt July. But it was necessary. It would be the last drop July's mother has done to hurt July. July decision was to tell her mother and her sister-in-law to stay away from her, to forget that she existed, and that she wasn't alone and to not twist her words because at the end they had to respond to God for what they were doing her. Two years passed, and they haven't tried to come close to July. And for her husband, he was also thrown away from the house. He was sleeping in his car. But one night he manages to get in the house. They got into a huge fight that he almost killed July by strangling her. July bit him on his shoulder to escape and called 911. After that, he was told to stay away from her and to leave the house.

Broken in pieces like she has never been before, July prayed to God to helped her to stay strong for her children and to find the light at the end of the tunnel because it looked so dark that it seemed like she's not going to make it. Little did she know that God's grace was so close, that she was going to be impressed with all the miracles he had on the way for her for being so strong and staying still when he said so.

CHAPTER 5

Grace

Finally, July found out that God is real. She always thought she knew, but like most people, there were doubts and needed proof. Indeed, she found him. After accepting God back in her life, things started to change. Once again her husband asked for forgiveness, that he didn't want to lose his family, and this time he would do whatever July wanted. For starters, he needed to go to church with her. This was hard for him because he is Catholic, he but agreed to go with her to the other church. He also liked it, and now they all go as a family every Sunday. Before July used to go alone with her kids, but God had promised her that it was going to change and it did. From then on God grace was just kept pouring down from heaven. They bought a new car. Likewise, God told her husband that he was going to have a better job position. July's husband asked to forgive him again, but this time for not believing in her that night and for not understanding that she was suffering and did what he did. They tried once again to apply for a house. This time July was without a job, but her brother decided to help her. And now they have a beautiful home. July decorated all the rooms, kitchen, living room, bedrooms with frames that have verses from the Bible. July believe that this house is a miracle from God. Submissive in God power, she wanted to say thanks to God every time she walks in any room by reading a verse. She also believes that this will help strengthen her relationship with God. The best of all miracles he did for her was that she didn't feel any sadness, anger, or fear in her heart now. There are no tears anymore, just happiness. God cleaned her heart. Let's not forget her two beautiful children that he has given to her and that he has protected them from July's sins. With that said, if this book saves one soul, it is worth the pain July went through. Only God knows how much you can take. He is not going to leave you stranded, just let him work his grace in you.

In conclusion, July talked about how God was there with her even in her darkest moments. Because otherwise, she could have been dead by now. God has been merciful and patient with July. She has much to thank him now. July learned in all this process that God was preparing her to be his only God. July's heart at the beginning had a hard time understanding and making sense of God's plan because she practically raised herself since she was little. Overall, God was there teaching her the way he always was putting people around to help her along the way. The best part of all is that July is not an alcoholic or a drug addict. She didn't turn crazy like most people wanted or didn't kill herself because there were many attempts to commit suicide. Everything changed when July started having this dreams and vision. It was when July realized that God was real. She kind had an idea that he was real, but like most people, she needed proof. But God was patient with July. He knew her way and never pushed her, and little by little he made her a stronger woman. In his eyes, she always was beautiful, not like the way she saw herself. He loves everyone the way they are, even with all your sins if you for real ask forgiveness. He is merciful and will forgive you. The secret for that is talking to him like he is your best friend. Tell him your problems. No matter how you are, ask him. For example, if you cry, he will cry with you. If you rap, he will rap with you. If you scream, he will scream with you. If you dance, he will dance with you. If you jump, God will jump with you. He loves the way you are. He is your maker. He knows you better than no one. July now calls him Daddy not God because he is her dad, her maker, and her best friend. To add up to the secret how to pray, when July prays, always she ask first for the Holy Spirit to come and touch her. Because without the Holy Spirit, no one can get to Jesus, and when Jesus sees the Holy Spirit working on a person, the doors of heaven would open, and that's when an intervention from the sky happen. It could be with angels coming from the sky. It could be Jesus give you powers like healing or to be a prophecy or having dreams and visions just like July. If at that moment it doesn't come through, just keep on trying. July is now thirty-two years old, and just now the Holy Spirit is working on her. Just be patient with him like he is with you, and remember this is a process. God knows your time. Believe in God, and miracles will come your way. Let God do anything he wants with you, and the impossible will happen.

ABOUT THE AUTHOR

July is stay-at-home mom for God has given her two beautiful children in the process to remain stronger in God's eyes. She is married to a man that is not perfect in her eyes, but she asks God every time to help him understand her or the other way around for July to understand him in order to have a healthy marriage

July likes to read cooking books and watch cooking shows.

For July always try to keep God in front of everything she does now, even when she walks around the house doing anything July is talking with God. It sounds weird, but she in love with him.

She goes to church, started reading the Bible, and writing a lot about what she understands when she finishes reading a verse. For this reason, July is writing this book because some of the verses that July had read made her understand that she wasn't the only one going through this tragic event alone, it also happened in Bible, to people in the past.

July tries to stay occupied in everything from cooking to gardening because the devil is always around trying to keep her away from God. Just like July said before, she tries to keep God in her mind in order to block anything bad coming her way.

July enjoys doing activities with her family. She always tries to keep them together. It is a battle, but July knows that with God everything is possible.

July has a lot of faith in God, Jesus, and the Holy Spirit. Amen.

CPSIA information can be obtained
at www.ICGtesting.com
Printed in the USA
LVHW040720170619
621442LV00001B/225